T0089531

Curious George's Dictionary

From the Editors of the American Heritage® Dictionaries

Illustrated in the style of H. A. Rey by Mary O'Keefe Young

Additional illustrations by H. A. Rey and in the style of H. A. Rey
by Anna Grossnickle Hines, Greg Paprocki, Vipah International, and Martha Weston

Clarion Books
An Imprint of HarperCollins*Publishers*
Boston   New York

Copyright © 2016, 2008 by HarperCollins Publishers. All rights reserved.

Curious George® is a registered trademark of HarperCollins Publishers.

All rights reserved. No part of this book may be used or reproduced in any manner whatsoever without written permission except in the case of brief quotations embodied in critical articles and reviews. For information, address HarperCollins Publishers, 195 Broadway, New York, NY 10007.

Visit our websites: curiousgeorge.com *and* clarionbooks.com

ISBN-13: 978-0-544-33665-0

Library of Congress Cataloging-in-Publication Data

Curious George's dictionary / from the editors of the American Heritage Dictionaries ; illustrated in the style of H.A. Rey by Mary O'Keefe Young... [et al.].
    p. cm.
 ISBN-13: 978-0-618-98649-1
 ISBN-10: 0-618-98649-9
 1. English language--Dictionaries, Juvenile. 2. Picture dictionaries, English--Juvenile literature. I. Young, Mary O'Keefe , ill.
  PE1629.C88 2008
  423'.1--dc22

                                                                2008009000

ISBN-13: 978-0-547-21272-2 (Canadian ed.)
ISBN-10: 0-547-21272-0 (Canadian ed.)

Cover and text design by Edda V. Sigurðardóttir

Manufactured in China

3 4 5 6 7 8 9 10 - SCP - 25 24 23

Contents

Foreword

For decades, Curious George has been delighting children with his insatiable curiosity. Now, with *Curious George's Dictionary,* he turns his curiosity to the exciting world of words. *Curious George's Dictionary* resounds with the vocabulary of the here-and-now world that children live in, but at the same time it draws them into a more expansive world beyond. In these pages, George explores a vivid and expansive palette of words both known (*girl, more, see, take*) and new (*admire, mountain, pouch, sentence*). These words have been carefully selected from the most frequently occurring words that all children should know in the preschool and primary years. This selection of words helps to ensure that, as children begin their journey through school, their grasp of the most important underlying concepts and the labels that represent those concepts is secure.

With your guidance, children can explore this new world along with George. Here I describe just a few of the ways in which you can encourage children's natural curiosity about the riches contained in *Curious George's Dictionary.* With little adjustment, you can use these same approaches for young children whose home language is not English. George's delight and charm extends to all children.

Introducing children to the dictionary. In a four-page story at the front of the dictionary, George receives *Curious George's Dictionary* as a birthday present. He and the man with the yellow hat look at the new book together. Reading through this story with children will help them to learn about alphabetical order and other important features of dictionaries, such as the fact that some words, like *wave,* can have more than one meaning—a wave in the ocean or the wave of a hand. You can let children decide when they are ready to read the story with you and in what order—each page stands on its own.

Pointing out words. When we speak, we do not leave "spaces" between words. Everything runs together. Because of this, young children's understanding of what words actually *are* comes from their experiences with print. You can support the development of this profoundly important insight by drawing your finger underneath each headword from left to right as you read it aloud. Then, as you read the sentence that uses the headword, draw your finger along under the sentence, occasionally stopping at individual words as you pronounce them.

Talking about words. Talking with young children as you browse through *Curious George's Dictionary* is one of the most important activities you can do. As you look at different words with children, they will point to whatever captures their attention, exclaim about it, and invariably ask questions about it. You can use these opportunities to clarify and extend children's understanding, to ask questions that further tickle their curiosity and expand their vocabulary. For example, as you discuss the entry for the word *early* you might ask, "Do *we* ever need to wake up *early* in the morning? How do we know from the picture that it is *early* in the morning?" For the word *real* you might ask, "How do we know that the zebra on the right is the *real* zebra?" For the word *choose,* "Are there more apples *in* the bowl or *out* of the bowl?" Point to other objects in the pictures that are not included in the dictionary and name them—in the picture for *city,* for example, you may point to and discuss the *bridge* and its purpose and the different *buildings,* which include *skyscrapers.*

On occasion, children will use a word other than the headword to name a picture—*fridge* instead of *refrigerator,* for example. In such situations you can simply say, "That's right!" and, pointing to the headword and reading it aloud, note that *"Refrigerator* is the *other* word that people use for *fridge."* Often children will use a more general or a more specific term for the picture—for example, *happy* instead of *smile.* This is an excellent opportunity to talk about how *happy* and *smile* are different but related—"You smile when you're happy." Whenever possible, provide an example of each and talk about the differences—"*Happy* is how you feel, and *smile* is what you do."

Teaching letters and sounds. Curious George's Dictionary provides a rich curriculum for teaching the names of the letters of the alphabet and for learning both their lower- and upper-case forms. As young children come to understand what a "word" is, they are better able to learn about and understand the relationship between those letters and sounds within words. Begin by talking about the sounds of letters like *b, m, r,* and *s,* and later move to vowel sounds and the letters that stand for them—*a, e, i, o,* and *u.* A conversation about the letter *s* and the sound it represents, for example, could go something like this: "Let's look at the words that begin with the letter *s.* Do they all begin with the same sound? Let's listen and see: *sad, ssss-ad . . . sit, ssss-it . . . soon, ssss-oon . . .* Do they sound like they all begin the same way?" Extend this by asking about *different* beginning letters and sounds: "*Cat* and *mud*—do they sound like they begin the same way?" And later still, it is valuable to show words to children and ask them to think of other words that are not in *Curious George's Dictionary*: "*Mud. Mmmm-ud.* What other things can we think of that begin with the *mmmm,* or "m" sound?" Use the alphabet page at the beginning of the book to talk about different letters.

Exploring categories of words. Seven special features at the back of the dictionary illustrate certain categories of words: numbers, calendar words, quantities, colors and shapes, location words, opposites, and question words. These features provide endless opportunities for interacting with children. On the numbers page, for example, pick a number and count the items together. On the calendar page, point out today's date or the child's birthday. Make a game of looking for red or square objects around the room. Ask if something is *under, over, in,* or *out.* Play an opposites game by covering up one half of the pair and having the child guess what it is you're hiding.

Encouraging writing. Most children want to write, just as they want to draw. Support this desire, but avoid emphasizing correct spelling— that will come later. It is enough for preschoolers to enjoy trying to write whatever they can, including copying words from *Curious George's Dictionary.* Many children will want to make their own dictionaries of their favorite words.

Our children are growing up in a digital world where books and the printed page may appear to be diminishing in importance. What will assuredly *not* diminish, however, is the power of snuggling with a child while sharing a book, or sitting on the floor with a group of children and reading aloud. There are treasures in this dictionary, and as you discover them with children in their here-and-now world you are inevitably and unerringly preparing them for the ways of the world beyond and yet to come.

—Shane Templeton

Foundation Professor of Literacy Studies
College of Education
University of Nevada, Reno

The Alphabet

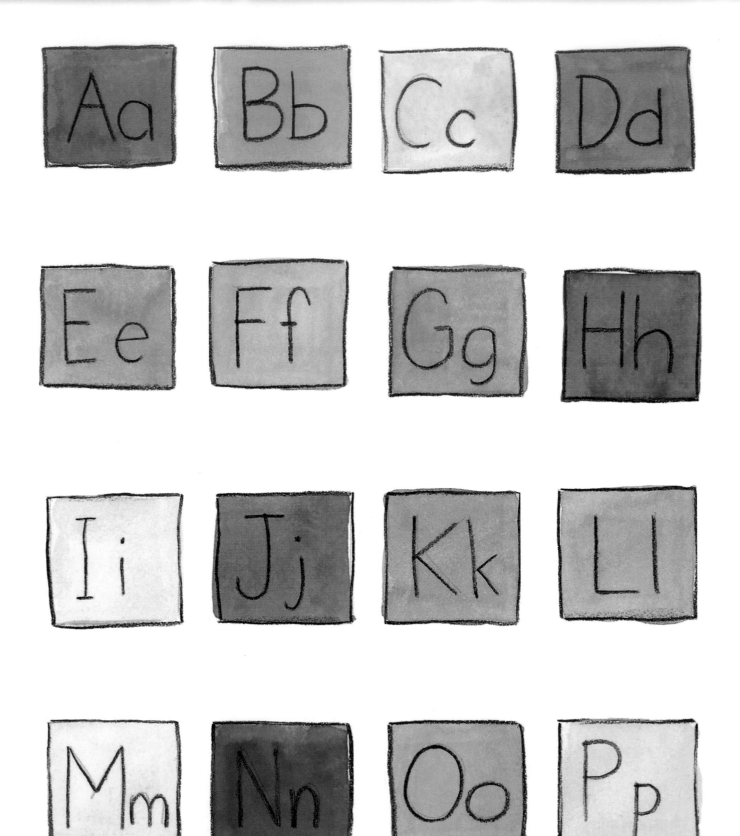

Aa Bb Cc Dd

Ee Ff Gg Hh

Ii Jj Kk Ll

Mm Nn Oo Pp

George Learns How to Use the Dictionary

George's Birthday

George is excited. Today is his birthday, and he has a present!

It's a big book full of words and pictures. This kind of book is a dictionary.

"Look!" says the man with the yellow hat. "You can learn all about different words in this book."

"Let's look for a word. Do you think we can find your favorite fruit?"

"Words that start with A come first. Z comes last. What letter does banana start with?"

"That's right! Banana starts with the letter B. Here it is! Let's spell it together."

Other fruits you can look for in your dictionary: apple, grapes, orange

George's Friends

George wants to find one of his animal friends, the kangaroo. Where will he find her?

"That's right," says the man with the yellow hat. "K comes after J and before L."

"Now we know where to find kangaroo."

"Let's see what other words start with K. The next word is keep. George keeps his toys in a box."

"Let's think of another sentence with keep. What does the kangaroo keep in her pouch?"

"That's right! The kangaroo keeps her baby in her pouch."

Other animals you can look for in your dictionary: alligator, cat, dog, penguin

George at the Beach

George and the man with the yellow hat are playing in the waves at the beach.

When George finds the word wave in the dictionary, he sees two different pictures!

One picture shows George riding on a wave in the ocean.

The other picture shows George waving his hand.

"That's right," says the man with the yellow hat. "There are two different kinds of wave in the dictionary."

"You can wave to me when you're playing in the waves!"

Now George is curious about what other words are in his new book.

He closes his eyes, opens the dictionary, and points to a word.

scamper
The mice scamper across the rug.

The word starts with S. The man with the yellow hat says the word and spells it. "Scamper. S-C-A-M-P-E-R."

What does the sentence say? "The mice scamper across the rug."

George is learning a new word! He wants to show that he knows the word. Now George is scampering, too!

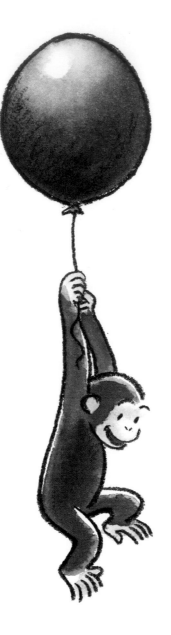

A B C D E F G H I J K L M N O P Q R S T U V W X Y Z
a b c d e f g h i j k l m n o p q r s t u v w x y z

about

The seal is **about** to eat the fish.

admire

George **admires** his new hat in the mirror.

afraid

George is **afraid**.

after

After eating all the fish, the seal is full.

afternoon

The man with the yellow hat comes home in the afternoon.

again

George tasted the cake. Now he is tasting it again!

ahead

George is ahead of the dog.

airplane

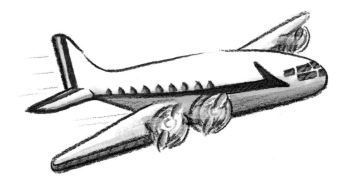

alligator

almost

It is almost time to start the race.

alone

One ant is alone.

always

George is always curious about something.

animals

another

The man with the yellow hat gives the rabbit another carrot.

answer

George knows the answer.

HOW MANY?

ant

apple

apron

are

The frogs **are** green.

arm

George is carrying an umbrella over his **arm**.

ask

The man with the yellow hat **asks** for a grape.

away

The balloon flies **away**.

Bb

A **B** C D E F G H I J K L M N O P Q R S T U V W X Y Z
a **b** c d e f g h i j k l m n o p q r s t u v w x y z

baby

back

The dog is in the back of the car.

bad

The medicine tastes bad.

bag

balance

George **balances** books on his head.

ball

balloons

banana

bath

beach

bean

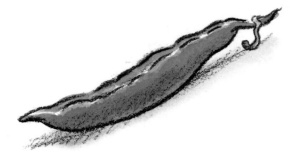

bed

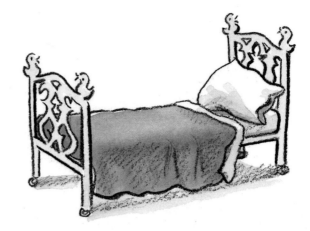

before

Before he goes outside, George puts on his hat.

bicycle

big

George holds a big heart.

bird

birthday

Today is George's **birthday**!

blanket

blow

George **blows** out the candles.

boat

body

George covers the man's **body** with sand.

book

George likes **books**.

boots

both

George covers **both** eyes.

bottle

bottom

George looks at the **bottom** of his foot.

bowl

box

boy

bread

break

The egg breaks.

breakfast

bring

George brings his ball.

bubbles

build

George builds a house.

bunny

bus

busy

The man with the yellow hat is too busy to play.

butterfly

buy

The man with the yellow hat buys some fruit.

C c

A B C D E F G H I J K L M N O P Q R S T U V W X Y Z
a b c d e f g h i j k l m n o p q r s t u v w x y z

cake

calendar

camel

camera

can
The beans are in a can.

can
George can paint.

candles

candy

cap

car

careful

George is careful when he pours the juice.

carrot

carry

George is carrying a big kite.

cat

catch

George catches the ball.

chair

change

The man with the yellow hat changes his socks.

chicken

choose

George chooses an apple.

chopsticks

The man with the yellow hat eats with chopsticks.

city

clean

Now the bicycle is clean.

27

climb

clock

close

George **closes** the window.

clothes

cloud

coat

cold

George's ears are cold!

color

The pumpkin and the carrot are the same color.

come

The cat comes inside.

computer

cook

cookie

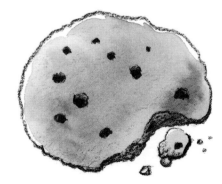

corn

couch

count

George **counts** the bunnies.

cover

George **covers** his eyes.

cow

crayons

cross

George **crosses** the road.

cry

curious

George is **curious** about what's inside the box.

curtains

curved

The road is **curved**.

cut

George **cuts** the cake.

D d

ABCDEFGHIJKLMNOPQRSTUVWXYZ
abcdefghijklmnopqrstuvwxyz

dance

George and the penguin **dance**.

dark

At night the sky is **dark**.

day

During the **day**, the sun shines.

decide

George **decides** which one to take.

deep

The water is deep.

desk

dictionary

different

The two flowers are different.

dig

The man with the yellow hat digs with a shovel.

dinner

dinosaur

dirty

Now the truck is **dirty**.

discover

They **discover** a bicycle inside the box.

dive

George **dives** into the water.

do

George is **doing** a puzzle.

dog

doll

door

down

George sleds **down** the hill.

draw

dream

George is **dreaming**.

dress

dresser

drink

George has a hot **drink**.

drive

drop

George **drops** some papers.

drums

dry

George is **drying** the plates.

E e

A B C D **E** F G H I J K L M N O P Q R S T U V W X Y Z
a b c d **e** f g h i j k l m n o p q r s t u v w x y z

each

George has something in **each** hand.

ear

The pencil is behind George's **ear**.

early

The baby bunny wakes up **early** in the morning.

easy

The puzzle is **easy**.

eat

George eats a banana.

egg

elephant

edge

George sits on the edge.

elbow

The man with the yellow hat hurt his elbow.

empty

enough

The giraffe is tall **enough** to reach the leaves.

escape

The dog **escapes** through the fence.

evening

The sun goes down in the **evening**.

every

George tries **every** color.

excited

George is **excited** to see the snow.

eyes

The cat has green **eyes**.

F f

A B C D E **F** G H I J K L M N O P Q R S T U V W X Y Z
a b c d e **f** g h i j k l m n o p q r s t u v w x y z

face

George has ice cream on his **face**.

fall

It is **fall**.

fall

They are **falling**.

far

The horse is **far** away.

fast

George is going **fast**.

favorite

George's **favorite** snack is a banana.

feather

fence

field

fill

George **fills** the dog's bowl.

find

George **finds** a hat.

finger

The man with the yellow hat points with his **finger**.

fire

George cooks over the **fire**.

first

George is **first**.

fish

fix

George **fixes** the fence.

float

The paper boat **floats** on the water.

flowers

fly

A **fly** is a kind of insect.

fly

The balloons **fly** away!

fold

George **folds** the paper.

follow

George **follows** the penguin.

food

foot

The man with the yellow hat puts a sock on his **foot**.

forget

George **forgets** to close the door.

fork

friend

The bunny is George's **friend**.

frog

front

The pictures are on the front of the refrigerator.

frown

The man with the yellow hat frowns.

fruit

full

fun

George has fun in the snow.

furniture

G g

A B C D E F **G** H I J K L M N O P Q R S T U V W X Y Z
a b c d e f **g** h i j k l m n o p q r s t u v w x y z

game

gate

get

George **gets** a present for his birthday.

giraffe

46

girl

give

The man with the
yellow hat gives
George some food.

glass

glasses

gloves

go

The cat goes outside.

good
The orange tastes good.

grab
George grabs the toy.

grapes

grow
Water helps the plants grow.

guess
George tries to guess where the bunny is hiding.

guitar

H h

A B C D E F G **H** I J K L M N O P Q R S T U V W X Y Z
a b c d e f g **h** i j k l m n o p q r s t u v w x y z

hair

The man with the yellow hat has black **hair**.

hand

George waves with his **hand**.

hang

George **hangs** from the balloons.

happy

The man with the yellow hat is **happy** to see George.

hard

The puzzle is hard.

hard

The ice is hard.

has

George has bananas.

hat

head

George puts a pillow on his head.

hear

The dog hears the telephone.

heavy

help

The man with the yellow hat helps **George.**

here

Here is the fruit.

hide

George hides.

high

George is very high.

hike

hill

hit

George **hits** the ball.

hold

George **holds** the string.

home

The man with the yellow hat comes **home**.

horse

hot

George is **hot**!

hour

The bread will be ready in one **hour**.

house

hug

hungry

The baby birds are **hungry**.

hurry

George is **hurrying** to catch the ball.

hurt

Ow! He **hurt** his knee.

I i

A B C D E F G H **I** J K L M N O P Q R S T U V W X Y Z
a b c d e f g h **i** j k l m n o p q r s t u v w x y z

ice

ice cream

idea

George has an idea for a trip.

important

It is important to give the dog water every day.

54

indoors

George stays indoors when it rains.

insects

instead

George wants a banana instead of an orange.

instruments

is

The car is blue.

island

J j

A B C D E F G H I **J** K L M N O P Q R S T U V W X Y Z
a b c d e f g h i **j** k l m n o p q r s t u v w x y z

jacket

juggle

juice

jump

K k

A B C D E F G H I J **K** L M N O P Q R S T U V W X Y Z
a b c d e f g h i j **k** l m n o p q r s t u v w x y z

kangaroo

keep

George **keeps** his toys in a box.

key

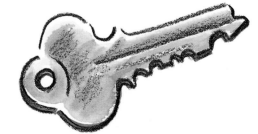

kick

George **kicks** the ball.

kind

The man with the yellow hat likes this **kind** of hat.

kiss

kite

knee

The man with the yellow hat is on one **knee**.

knife

know

George **knows** how to spell his name.

L l

A B C D E F G H I J K **L** M N O P Q R S T U V W X Y Z
a b c d e f g h i j k **l** m n o p q r s t u v w x y z

lake

lamp

land

The boat is near the land.

large

last

George is last.

late

George is late for the bus.

laugh

leaf

lean

George leans back.

learn

George learns the alphabet.

leave

The man with the yellow hat **leaves** his umbrella near the door.

left

The arrow points to the **left**.

leg

The horse lifts one **leg**.

less

There is **less** milk in the green glass than in the blue glass.

let

George **lets** the elephant eat from his hand.

letters

lettuce

library

lie

The cat **lies** in the sun.

lift

George **lifts** the bunny.

light

The empty boxes are **light**.

light

The **light** from the moon shines in the window.

like

George **likes** the spider.

lion

listen

George **listens** to the bird singing.

little

There is only a **little** milk in the glass.

live

The frogs **live** in the pond.

long

The kangaroo has a **long** tail.

look

George **looks** out the window.

lose

The man with the yellow hat **loses** his hat.

loud

love

George **loves** to climb trees.

low

The bird is **low** in the tree.

lunch

M m

A B C D E F G H I J K L **M** N O P Q R S T U V W X Y Z
a b c d e f g h i j k l **m** n o p q r s t u v w x y z

machine

mail

make

George **makes** a cake.

man

many

George has **many** bananas.

meat

medicine

meet

The two squirrels **meet** at the bottom of the tree.

mess

middle

The flowers are in the **middle** of the table.

milk

minute

The egg cooks for ten **minutes**.

mirror

miss

George **missed** the ball!

mittens

mix

money

moon

more

There is more milk in the blue glass than in the green glass.

morning

The sun comes up in the morning.

mountain

mouse

mouth

George puts the straw in his **mouth**.

move

The man with the yellow hat **moves** near the fire.

movie

mud

The pig is in the **mud**.

mug

music

The animals listen to the **music**.

N n

A B C D E F G H I J K L M **N** O P Q R S T U V W X Y Z
a b c d e f g h i j k l m **n** o p q r s t u v w x y z

name

narrow

The red ribbon is narrow.

near

The house is near the ocean.

neat

Now the room is neat and clean.

neck

George has a scarf around his **neck**.

need

George **needs** a spoon.

nest

never

The bunny **never** climbs trees.

new

George chooses a **new** cap.

next

The pig and the sheep are **next** to each other.

night

At night, the moon shines.

noise

George likes to make noise.

nose

The seal balances a ball on its nose.

nothing

There is nothing in the bowl.

now

Now it is time to go to sleep.

numbers

A B C D E F G H I J K L M N **O** P Q R S T U V W X Y Z
a b c d e f g h i j k l m n **o** p q r s t u v w x y z

ocean

offer

George **offers** a carrot to the bunny.

old

George chooses his **old** cap.

only

There is **only** one crayon in the box.

73

open

George **opens** the box.

opposite

The frog and the alligator are on **opposite** sides of the river.

orange

other

The squirrel is in the **other** tree.

outdoors

George plays **outdoors**.

own

George has his **own** chair.

P p

A B C D E F G H I J K L M N O **P** Q R S T U V W X Y Z
a b c d e f g h i j k l m n o **p** q r s t u v w x y z

page

George looks at a **page** of the book.

paint

George **paints** an egg.

pajamas

pants

paper

park

party

pat

George **pats** the dog.

paw

The cat puts its **paw** in the water.

peek

George **peeks** through the books.

peel

George **peels** a banana.

pen

pencil

penguin

pet

The **pets** sleep on George's bed.

petal

The flower has five **petals**.

phone

piano

pick

George **picks** an apple.

picnic

picture

piece

George takes one **piece**.

pig

pillow

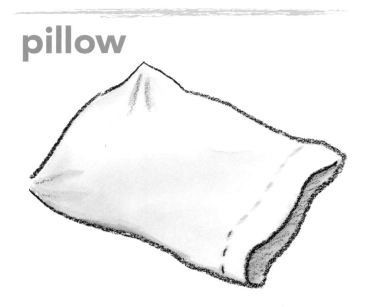

plant

plate

play

George **plays** **with the pieces.**

playground

point

George is pointing.

pond

pot

pouch

The baby kangaroo is in the pouch.

pour

present

puddle

pull

George **pulls** the chair out.

pumpkin

push

George **pushes** the chair in.

put

George **puts** the hat on.

puzzle

Qq

A B C D E F G H I J K L M N O P **Q** R S T U V W X Y Z

a b c d e f g h i j k l m n o p **q** r s t u v w x y z

question

The man with the yellow hat asks a **question**.

quick

The rabbit is **quick**!

quiet

George is trying to be **quiet**.

quilt

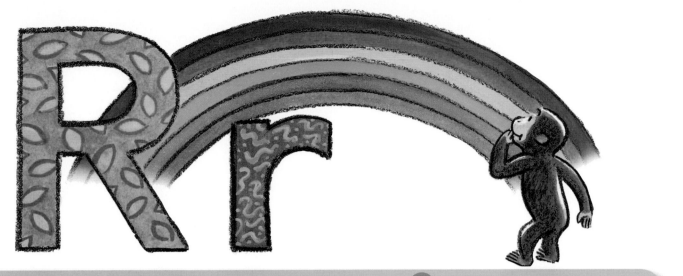

R r

A B C D E F G H I J K L M N O P Q **R** S T U V W X Y Z
a b c d e f g h i j k l m n o p q **r** s t u v w x y z

rabbit

race

rain

rainbow

reach

George **reaches** for the ball.

read

ready

George is **ready** to eat.

real

The one on the right is a **real** zebra.

refrigerator

remember

The man with the yellow hat **remembers** his keys.

rest

George **rests**.

ribbon

ride

George **rides** his bicycle.

right

That's **right**! D comes after C.

right

The arrow points to the **right**.

THIS WAY ➡
TO THE MONKEYS

river

road

rock

roof

The house has a red roof.

room

George has his own room.

rug

run

George runs on the beach.

S s

A B C D E F G H I J K L M N O P Q R **S** T U V W X Y Z
a b c d e f g h i j k l m n o p q r **s** t u v w x y z

sad

George is sad that it is raining.

same

The two flowers are the same.

sand

George plays in the sand.

say

The man with the yellow hat is saying "follow me!"

scamper

The mice scamper across the rug.

scarf

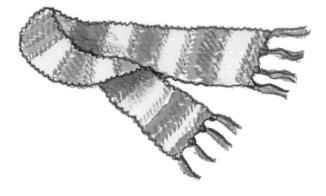

school

scissors

scratch

George scratches his head.

seal

secret

The present is a **secret**.

see

George can **see** far away.

sell

The woman **sells** fruit.

sentence

shadow

shake

The dog **shakes** water all over.

share

George **shares** his snack with the kangaroo.

sharp

The knife is **sharp**.

sheep

sheet

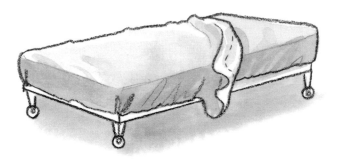

shine

The sun **shines** through the clouds.

shirt

shoes

shop

George **shops** for candy.

short

The jacket is too **short**.

shorts

should

George **should** put away his toys.

shovel

show

George **shows** the present to his friend.

shut

The man with the yellow hat **shuts** the gate.

sick

George is **sick** today.

side

The man with the yellow hat paints the **side** of the house.

sidewalk

sign

LIBRARY

sing

The man with the yellow hat likes to **sing**.

sit

skirt

sky

sled

George **sleds** in the winter.

sleep

George **sleeps** outdoors.

slide

George **slides** down the giraffe's neck.

slow

The penguin is **slow**.

small

George is too **small** to drive.

smell

The man with the yellow hat **smells** the flower.

smile

snack

George eats a **snack**.

snake

snow

soap

socks

soft

The snow is **soft**.

some

George has **some** of the bananas.

something

There is **something** under the rug.

sometimes

Sometimes George walks on his hands.

soon

Dinner will be ready **soon**.

sorry

George is **sorry**.

sound

What's that **sound**?

spell

George can **spell** the word d-o-g.

spider

spill

George will **spill** the food.

spin

splash

spoon

spring

It is **spring**.

squeeze

George **squeezes** the eggs.

squirrel

stand

George **stands** up.

stars

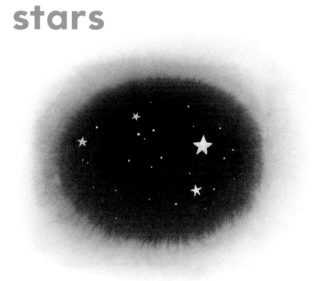

start

George **starts** to eat.

stay

The cat **stays** in the house.

steps

stomach

George pats the dog's **stomach**.

stop

store

storm

story

The man with the yellow hat reads a **story**.

stove

straight

The road is straight.

straw

street

string

subway

summer

It is **summer**.

sun

surprise

sweater

swim

swing

George **swings** in the tree.

A B C D E F G H I J K L M N O P Q R S **T** U V W X Y Z
a b c d e f g h i j k l m n o p q r s **t** u v w x y z

table

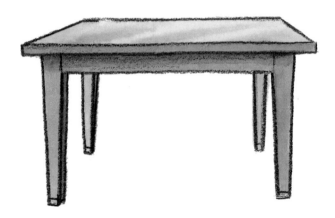

tail

The horse has a white tail.

take

George takes a piece of cake.

talk

The man with the yellow hat talks on the telephone.

tall

The man with the yellow hat is tall.

taste

George tastes the cake.

teach

The man with the yellow hat teaches George.

telephone

television

tell

The man with the yellow hat tells George to sit down.

thank

The man **thanks** George for the present.

there

There are the vegetables.

think

George **thinks** about what to draw.

thirsty

The dog is **thirsty**.

throw

George **throws** the leaves.

thumb

tie

George **ties** the string.

time

It is **time** to eat.

tired

George goes to bed when he is **tired**.

toe

George hangs from his **toes**.

together

They are walking **together**.

too

George is sleeping, **too**.

top

George is on **top** of the ball.

touch

George **touches** the ball.

towel

toy

George plays with his new **toy.**

train

tree

trip

George is going on a **trip**.

truck

turn

George **turns** his cap around.

trouble

Now George is in **trouble**.

try

George is **trying** to catch a fish.

TV

U u

A B C D E F G H I J K L M N O P Q R S T **U** V W X Y Z
a b c d e f g h i j k l m n o p q r s t **u** v w x y z

umbrella

until

George plays **until** dinner time.

up

George is going **up** the hill.

use

The man with the yellow hat **uses** a knife to open the box.

V v

A B C D E F G H I J K L M N O P Q R S T U **V** W X Y Z
a b c d e f g h i j k l m n o p q r s t u **v** w x y z

vacation

They are leaving for a **vacation**.

vegetables

very

The kite is **very** high.

visit

George **visits** his friends at the pond.

Ww

A B C D E F G H I J K L M N O P Q R S T U V **W** X Y Z
a b c d e f g h i j k l m n o p q r s t u v **w** x y z

wait

The dog **waits** for food.

wake

George **wakes** up.

walk

want

George **wants** some candy.

110

warn

The man with the yellow hat **warns** George.

wash

watch

George **watches** a butterfly.

water

wave

George rides on a **wave**.

wave

George is **waving**.

wear

He is **wearing** a yellow hat.

wet

The penguin is **wet**.

wheel

George rides on one **wheel**.

when

The man with the yellow hat wears an apron **when** he cooks.

whisper

wide

The yellow ribbon is **wide**.

will

George will throw the ball.

win

The bunny wins the race.

wind

window

winter

It is winter.

wish

George makes a wish.

woman

wonder

George **wonders** what is in the box.

word

This sentence has five words.

work

George is ready to **work**.

write

George **writes**.

wrong

No, that hat is the **wrong** color.

114

ABCDEFGHIJKLMNOPQRSTUVW**X**YZ
abcdefghijklmnopqrstuvw**x**yz

x-ray

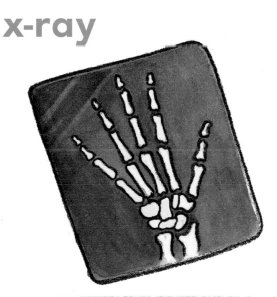

xylophone

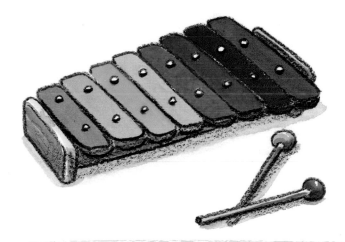

Y y

A B C D E F G H I J K L M N O P Q R S T U V W X **Y** Z
a b c d e f g h i j k l m n o p q r s t u v w x **y** z

yard

yawn

George **yawns**.

young

The horse is **young**.

yo-yo

116

Z z z

A B C D E F G H I J K L M N O P Q R S T U V W X Y **Z**
a b c d e f g h i j k l m n o p q r s t u v w x y **z**

zebra

zigzag

George **zigzags** down the hill.

zipper

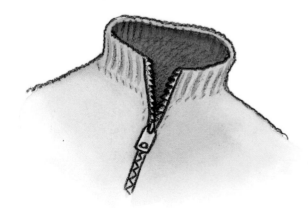

zoo

Numbers

1 banana

2 beds

3 dogs

4 zebras

5 leaves

6 umbrellas

7 frogs

8 rabbits

9 mugs

10 penguins

11 pumpkins

12 camels

13 kites

14 balls

15 giraffes

16 caps

17 flowers

18 ants

19 apples

20 hats

Practicing Counting

How many marshmallows is George cooking?

How many bunnies are there?

How many balloons does George have?

How many apples are in the tree?

Calendar

Year

January
Monday	Tuesday	Wednesday	Thursday	Friday	Saturday	Sunday
		1	2	3	4	5
6	7	8	9	10	11	12
13	14	15	16	17	18	19
20	21	22	23	24	25	26
27	28	29	30	31		

February
Monday	Tuesday	Wednesday	Thursday	Friday	Saturday	Sunday
					1	2
3	4	5	6	7	8	9
10	11	12	13	14	15	16
17	18	19	20	21	22	23
24	25	26	27	28		

March
Monday	Tuesday	Wednesday	Thursday	Friday	Saturday	Sunday
					1	2
3	4	5	6	7	8	9
10	11	12	13	14	15	16
17	18	19	20	21	22	23
24/31	25	26	27	28	29	30

April
Monday	Tuesday	Wednesday	Thursday	Friday	Saturday	Sunday
	1	2	3	4	5	6
7	8	9	10	11	12	13
14	15	16	17	18	19	20
21	22	23	24	25	26	27
28	29	30				

May
Monday	Tuesday	Wednesday	Thursday	Friday	Saturday	Sunday
			1	2	3	4
5	6	7	8	9	10	11
12	13	14	15	16	17	18
19	20	21	22	23	24	25
26	27	28	29	30	31	

June
Monday	Tuesday	Wednesday	Thursday	Friday	Saturday	Sunday
						1
2	3	4	5	6	7	8
9	10	11	12	13	14	15
16	17	18	19	20	21	22
23/30	24	25	26	27	28	29

July
Monday	Tuesday	Wednesday	Thursday	Friday	Saturday	Sunday
	1	2	3	4	5	6
7	8	9	10	11	12	13
14	15	16	17	18	19	20
21	22	23	24	25	26	27
28	29	30	31			

August
Monday	Tuesday	Wednesday	Thursday	Friday	Saturday	Sunday
				1	2	3
4	5	6	7	8	9	10
11	12	13	14	15	16	17
18	19	20	21	22	23	24
25	26	27	28	29	30	31

September
Monday	Tuesday	Wednesday	Thursday	Friday	Saturday	Sunday
1	2	3	4	5	6	7
8	9	10	11	12	13	14
15	16	17	18	19	20	21
22	23	24	25	26	27	28
29	30					

October
Monday	Tuesday	Wednesday	Thursday	Friday	Saturday	Sunday
		1	2	3	4	5
6	7	8	9	10	11	12
13	14	15	16	17	18	19
20	21	22	23	24	25	26
27	28	29	30	31		

November
Monday	Tuesday	Wednesday	Thursday	Friday	Saturday	Sunday
					1	2
3	4	5	6	7	8	9
10	11	12	13	14	15	16
17	18	19	20	21	22	23
24	25	26	27	28	29	30

December
Monday	Tuesday	Wednesday	Thursday	Friday	Saturday	Sunday
1	2	3	4	5	6	7
8	9	10	11	12	13	14
15	16	17	18	19	20	21
22	23	24	25	26	27	28
29	30	31				

Month

September
Monday	Tuesday	Wednesday	Thursday	Friday	Saturday	Sunday
1	2 Party Today!	3	4	5	6	7
8	9	10	11	12	13	14
15	16	17	18	19	20	21
22	23	24	25	26	27	
29	30					

Quantities

none

George has **none** of the bananas.

a few

George has **a few** of the bananas.

half

George has **half** of the bananas.

most

George has **most** of the bananas.

all

George has **all** of the bananas.

Colors and Shapes

blue star

yellow circle

gray sphere

green rectangle

brown square

red heart

black arrow

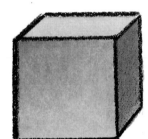

pink cube

orange triangle

purple diamond

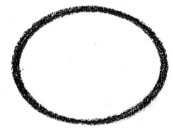

white oval

Location Words

to

from

out

in

off

on

inside

behind

around

outside

in front

above

with

over

below

under

across

along

between

beside

through

Opposites

short **tall** **small** **big**

wide **narrow** **stop** **go**

light **heavy** **hot** **cold**

empty **full** **sad** **happy**

Question Words

Who is walking with George?
What happens to the hat?
Where does the hat go?

Why is George in the tree?
How does he get there?
Which animal helps him?